Copyright © 2018 Eric K. Lai

All rights reserved.

ISBN: 978-0-6482217-9-1

First Edition

Published by Happy Logic Creations

A catalogue record for this book is available from the National Library of Australia

Dedication

This book is dedicated to my beautiful daughter Adorna, who always inspire me to become a better person and allowing me to find my key to the universe.

Eric K. Lai

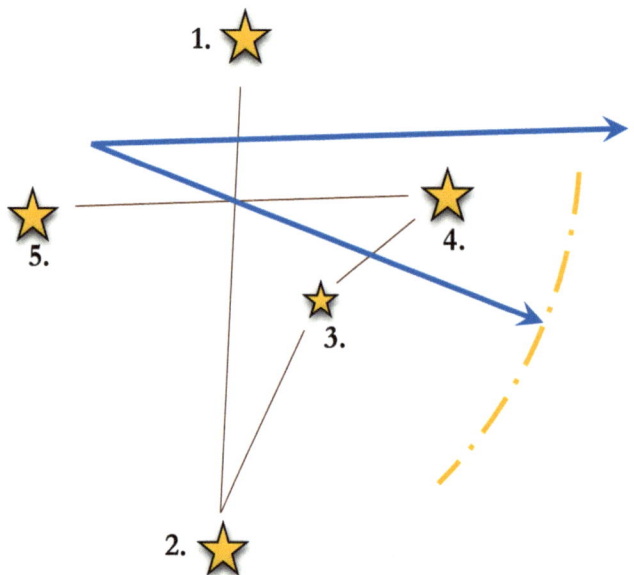

Contents

Acknowledgments vii

1. Heaven, Earth and everything in between 9
2. You were put here for a reason 10
3. God and star dust 11
4. Understand your personal lock 14
5. Key to the universe 16
6. Leave a positive legacy 18
7. Mirror what is good in this world 19
8. Locate your universal anchor 21
9. Winners, Losers and Grinners 23
10. Embrace our Future 25

About the author 26

Eric K. Lai

Acknowledgments

I would like to acknowledge the Traditional Owners of the land on which this book was written and pay my respects to their Elders both past and present.

Eric K. Lai

1. Heaven, Earth and everything in between

This book is about engineering relationships between Heaven, Earth and Humanity

Engineering in the basic sense is utilising methodical approaches in order to create something of value. When I talk about engineering relationships, I am talking about successfully combining your lifestyle, experience and personality into a key which fits into (or relates to) the way you view Heaven, Earth and everything in between within this universe.

It may seem daunting to think that such a key to the universe exists, but we each hold one within ourselves. It is like an heirloom that has passed down from our ancestors which originated from the early formation of universe. The idea is to know what your personal lock is and find that key which can unlock your own universal secrets.

Heaven is a glorious place beyond Earth. It is within the stars and planets, A unique uncorrupted version of beauty more perfect than ours, which we are incapable of travelling to physically.
Different religions have different definition however, but they all share a common theme in that we are still able to communicate with this place or realm.

Earth is where life survives and humanity coexist. Everything that happens on the planet eventually propagates and affect the surroundings. There is a saying that everybody needs and relies on another person in one way or another, which goes "no man (or woman) is an island".

The medium that binds Heaven and Earth is the spirit from God or supernatural forces. Everyone has the capability to receive these, but not many know how to utilise it to achieve universal oneness and harmony. This book will bridge that gap and will be an introduction as a guide on how to allow your inner human spirit to establish a communications link between Heaven and Earth.

2. You were put here for a reason

You are as important and brilliant as the stars. This is because you contain material which originally came from the universe. That is, you have cosmological compounds inside you which is as ancient as the star dust created from miraculous explosions billions of years ago. You are made eligible and have all prerequisites to communicate with Heaven and Earth. You have a purpose to fulfil as a descendant of the cosmos.

Realise however, there are things in this world that are beyond our control. A bird can only fly as high as its own ability and shape that is given, so don't stress over things which others can accomplish but you cannot. You are unique for a reason. Embrace our future and discover your destiny by seeking your key to the universe.

As mentioned previously there is Heaven (celestial place or spiritual realm) and Earth. A famous Asian hip-hop friend Jin Au-Yeung (also known as MC Jin) have said in a track from the album XIV:LIX the reason for your existence is "it can't be to just eat, sleep, and die". The question I believe he is asking is what is your reason to live? What is your role in the big scheme of things?

First you need understand a notion that randomness is a secondary effect to purposeful and intelligent design. The intelligent design in this case is your physical body and the non-physical part is emotions, soul and spirit. The randomness is within your DNA. You may have black hair, dark skin and be very happy or you may have blue eyes, white skin and are always grumpy. As everyone have a unique path and destiny, I'm not discriminating which is better, but just highlighting the fact that randomness is inherited by design. Otherwise we will become clones of each other with no individual identity. This would be extremely confusing and will lead to undesirable consequences.

Even with a current total population of more than 7 billion people in this world, you have a reason to be here. Make the most of your given opportunities and take advantage of good fortunes that comes your way. You are not an accident created by random. When you realise the epic sacrifices others have made to get you to this moment in life, you will understand that wishes do come true!

3. God and star dust

Everything in the universe was created from the big bang. Why should DNA be any different?

Those that believe in the big bang theory will know that the universe came from a point in space and time approximately 13.7 billion of solar years ago. Where did all that material come from? Well the theory is that it existed as a pulsating supermassive build-up of quantum fluctuations immediately prior to the big explosion.

The good news is, you are part of the material that came from it. In another words, your DNA has rearranged elements that ultimately are part of the earliest possible star clouds. Creation was done in stages and one interpretation is that God initiated the big bang. Given that all the initial conditions and circumstances of the big bang cannot be replicated, there will ever be only one of you and one of me in this universe! Humanity cannot recreate their own exact self or be able to reverse a cooked egg back to its raw state. Time flows like water running down the mountain.

The Book of Genesis, which is the first book of the Bible, begins with the creation of the world. God is the creator of our world. In Hebrew, the meaning of "Genesis" is the Book of Beginnings. This is because many new beginnings are recorded in Genesis. Genesis is actually the first book of the Law of Moses or "Torah" which is actually the first five books of the Bible. There are seven periods of creation recorded in the beginning of Genesis. Although each of these has been translated as a "day", the original Hebrew word used before translation is "yom" which simply means a period of time with a beginning and an ending.

It is unlikely to be a solar day since the sun, moon and stars did not appear until the fourth "day".

The periods of time as recorded are as follows:

    One: Night and day distinction.
    Two: Sky and sea separation.
    Three: Land and vegetation developed.
    Four: Stars, sun and moon formed as the world begins to rotate.
    Five: Sea creatures including fish and birds developed.
    Six: God placed man (and women) in the world, and allowed them to rule over the animals.
    Seven: Period of rest.

You may not necessarily believe in God, but I'm certain that you know there are subjects and celestial objects that are beyond this world.

The Jewel Box cluster with the ESO VLT
(View from Southern Hemisphere)

The Solar System

Our Home Planet

4. Understand your personal lock

The second notion is that there is a personal lock hidden away within yourself which leads you to your treasure box and destiny. The destiny I am referring to is the way or purpose which you set out to fulfil in your life. It is important to identify what this lock is as you will need to be able to unlock it to achieve your vision. It may be something is causing you to bottle up all your negative feelings leading to confusion and anger, or giving you trouble and anxiety. Holding on to too much hardship is harmful to your health. Although it is considered human to experience it, eventually you will need to be release that lock to feel free. It may be that there is something which is preventing you to become better. You want to move on, but don't know how or where to begin.

To change your circumstances, you should understand what your personal lock is and how to unlock it. To do so, you need to use the special key to the universe. It will enable perspective and give clarity to something which may seem fuzzy. Where can find and obtain this key? I'm glad you asked… It is something that money cannot buy. The good news is it is already infused in your soul and you already own it!

This book will guide you to uncover what keys to the universe are and how to extract your own personal one. Using the key to the universe will turn negativity into something positive, constructive and valuable. It is helpful and essential for wanting to create happy logic.

COMMUNICATING WITH HEAVEN AND EARTH

5. Key to the universe

It may seem daunting to think that such a key to the universe exists, but we each have our own within ourselves. It is inherited from the DNA and molecules that come from the early formation of the universe. The challenge is to know what your personal lock is and how to find your key which can unlock your own universal secrets.

Why would you want to use a key that has a link to the universe? Good question dear inquisitive one… It is because the cosmos and the stars is fundamentally imbedded to our soul which we are all part of. We want to reach out for things and explore what is beyond us. To seek inspiration from things unseen, and to achieve goals that does not yet exist on this planet.

Meditation or praying may help with seeking clarity on issues affecting your life. However it is very important to allocate quiet and uninterrupted time to find your key to the universe. It could give you the answers you seek as well as remind you to appreciate the simple things in life. A quiet soul allows for inner peace and lets you connect your spirit with the universe. This will lead you to search and pick the stars in the night sky which shall be used as your guide. Isolate and note your selection based on which stars inspires you and whether there exists a sense of personal connection. When you have your group of stars, join them to together by connecting them in lines that form a reproducible pattern. This shape or form will then become your star signature.

A star signature is the graphical form or visual representation for your key to the universe, it forms half of the full key. Here is an example of my own star signature shown below:

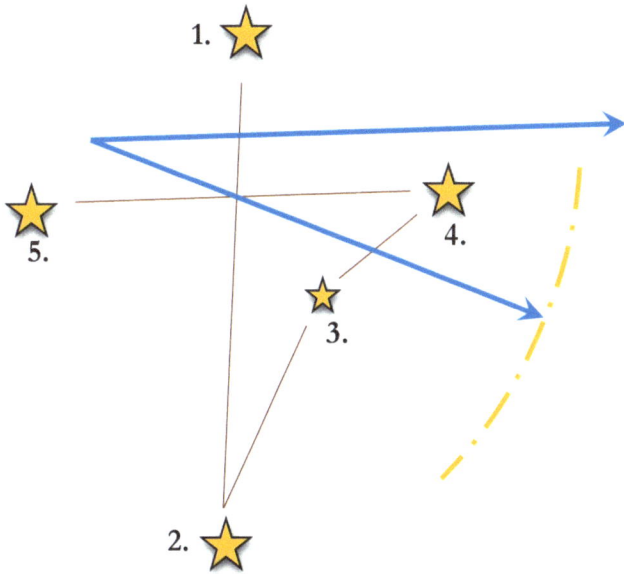

With such a vast number of stars in the universe, you will be able to find, locate and create a star signature to for your use. The next few chapters highlight what to incorporate or consider to when establishing your key to the universe.

6. Leave a positive legacy

Leave a legacy of love and respect. What do you want to be remembered for? Do you want to be known as someone who promotes peace, upholds values and relationships, or someone who takes risks and achieves big rewards? As mentioned, everyone is special and most want to achieve something better.

The truth is what you do makes who you are and how you are seen. Even if you have a doctor's degree but choose to be an airline pilot, they will refer to you as "Captain, Officer or Pilot" but not "Doctor". For example, in the past I have worked as a qualified engineer in large companies such as Boeing Aerospace and Ford Motor company. Due to work shortages I changed career and started working in information technology as a service consultant. People including those close to me no longer called me "An engineer", and instead refers to me as "The computer guy".

How do you want to be addressed? What legacy would you like to leave, and whom do you want to be known to? It is not too late to consolidate your skills, talents and assets to move in the direction that gets you closer to your dreams and aspirations.

You can be happy today !

7. Mirror what is good in this world

Imitate the good deeds. Think big and feel free to dream. Many great inventions and inspiration come from people who dare to dream and think outside the normal patterns or repetitive cycles. Don't be afraid to see who is good in this world and mirror their strengths. This can be from any person whether they have scientific or artistic skills, as long as it is of benefit to the overall community. When you have found your influencer, make sure you don't lose sight of your own personality and vision. You'll still need to have your own unique personality and be able to make use of something that could contribute to a legacy.

Remember not everything is to be seen as polar (meaning either positive or negative) or black and white. Even if you are stuck on one side that is not good, it won't be forever. Time heals many emotional or psychological pain. Things will eventually change just like the seasons. After dark experiences, there will always be bright ones. Even the famous and important yin-yang symbol does not have any distinct straight start and finish lines. It is curved, complementary and in harmony. I see it like a dance between the light and dark forces of nature.

The Yin and Yang Symbol often used in Tai Chi

8. Locate your universal anchor

Everything can have Heaven-Earth relationships. Remember the star signature you created before? Your visual knowledge and understanding behind it is known as the "Heaven link".

There is also an "Earth link" which is essentially knowledge in this world that is of interest to you. Your Earth link for communication can come from historical works, religious preference, spiritual and metaphysical realm, celestial art or space themes. For example you can consider the following areas of interest:

In the bible:
[Genesis 1:16 English Standard Version (ESV)]
"And God made the two great lights—the greater light to rule the day and the lesser light to rule the night—and the stars."
The writer Moses is referring to the sun, the moon and the stars.

(As a comparison in the Quran by Muhammad):
[Quran 16:12] "And He commits, in your service, the night and the day, as well as the sun and the moon. Also, the stars are committed by His command. These are (sufficient) proofs for people who understand."

From Star Wars:
"May the Force be with you" has a connotations similar to Taoism with the connectedness between the light and dark sides has as in the yin and yang. The energy or spiritual force used is like Chi.

Or famous playwriter Shakespeare in Julius Caesar:
[Cassius] "The fault, dear Brutus, is not in our stars, but in ourselves."

If you have an area of interest that "clicks" or "resonates" with you, then use it as long as it has a relationship that is compatible with your star signature. The Earth link should enable you to connect with something heavenly that is associated with our world. I recommend selecting an area you enjoy which relates to something celestial, stellar, spiritual or even supernatural otherwise you will end up having to take the long route when reconciling with your knowledge of Heaven. Everyone is different, and will identify with different links to form their personal key for unlocking their personal lock.

The Heaven link and Earth link combines to form Heaven-Earth relationships. This is your universal anchor and is the other half of your key to the universe. It allows association of anything in between to be "anchored" back to a connection on Earth you are familiar with. Think of it as a safe "go to" foundation. You can have a universal anchor that acts as a focal point when communicating and then be able to fall back to familiarity when you become uncomfortable. The purpose is to prevent you from venturing too far and getting lost when communicating with Heaven.

The key to the universe can be simplified and defined using conceptual blocks as shown below:

Heaven link   = Your star signature knowledge.
Earth link   = Your Earth knowledge of interest relatable to something beyond our world.
Universal anchor   = Your Heaven link and Earth link or Heaven-Earth relationships.

Your key to the universe
    is your star signature & your universal anchor.
    = your star signature & Heaven link and Earth link.
    = (your star signature & your star signature knowledge) and Earth link.
    = (Heaven link) and (Earth link)

Note: Your star signature (in visual form) & your star signature knowledge (in mind form) merges to become your Heaven link only when both are reconciled together.

My universal anchor is The Holy Trinity whom transcends space-time. My mother's anchor is Jesus who's done everything between Heaven and Earth. My wife's Heaven link is the Southern Cross constellation (like mine). My daughter's Earth link is music and day dreaming as well as playing all she likes. My father's Heaven-Earth relationship is dragons from outside Earth which he believes once existed here.

You are free to choose what you like as the link within the Heaven-Earth relationship. If it is identifiable, relatable and significantly good for you, then use it to bind your star signature & your universal anchor together. This unique combination is personal to you and is your key to the universe.

When you finally find out what your key to the universe is, trust it to lead you to your treasure box and destiny. Use it appropriately to unlock communication with Heaven and Earth and utilise it to find direction and sense of purpose. Remember to continuously refer back to it in both visual and mind forms. You can then connect your spirit and project your mind to your star signature, relying on your universal anchor to bring you safely home if you lose your way. Your key becomes functional when you begin to succeed in creating happy logic!

9. Winners, Losers and Grinners

Being a winner means that someone or something had lost. You had beat someone else for a higher position or to win a game. If you understand not everyone can be winners (for example in wealth or opportunity) then you will not lose sleep if universal equality and freedom cannot be achieved.

Let me clarify with a question…

If freedom is the power or right to act, speak, or think as one wants, will there ever be a place where "one size fits all rules" can apply without repression or fear of oppression?

The answer is No. As such universal freedom is impossible by definition. There is no such thing as one size fits all. You may have freedom of choice, but realise freedom of speech and freedom of religious or cultural choice cannot be applied uniformly. For example, you can choose who you'd like to marry, but not all religions will allow same sex marriage. Are those that have firm teachings discriminating against those that have freedom of choice? Can a Chinese take away shop be forced to sell Italian food if the law says it must cater to all nationality? Will it be discriminating or insulting if no other cultural food is available in its shop?. I would say no. It is unrealistic to expect all places cater to all different types of people. Again no such thing as "one size fits all", or "one shop caters all". You just need to find the right key to unlock your part of the universe.

What I am saying is that it is statistically impossible to have universal laws that can be enforced on everyone without compromising on free will or speech.

There will always be winners, losers and grinners. Losers can eventually be winners, and winners may have a change in fortune and become losers. The safest and best option in my humble opinion are those who always smile in all circumstances.

10. Embrace our Future

The future will always move ahead faster than you least expect. If you don't want to do anything about it, somebody else will. Time is limited and will eventually catch up with us all. So act today to achieve your goals and dreams rather than procrastinate and start later. Do something which you will be proud of in ten years' time and would be a lovely story to tell others, especially to younger generations. When communicating with Heaven and Earth during your lifetime, please have an open mind with a heart of always wanting to learn more. New things are always to be discovered at any age. Nobody knows everything or can see all perspectives. There are always at least two parts and sides to a story.

Thank you all for reading. I really hope that you will find your key to the universe. I shall leave you with some of my best inspirational quotes:

*"The ability to Imagine and Dream is a right, not a choice...
No one is allowed to take them away from you."*

- Nov 2013

"It takes a special someone to know someone special. Like minds think alike. Everybody is good at something, even if nobody has the ability to recognise it."

- Dec 2014

"We all live in this world, therefore we are already united in a physical sphere."

- Jan 2015

*"Destiny is a path set in Heaven by God.
We all have a piece of the universe in us,
and being able to cross paths with stars is pure bliss..."*

- March 2015

*"Happiness is saved in your heart.
The more you accumulate of it, the more that you can use later in life..."*

- Feb 2018

About the author

Eric is a passionate believer in all things that brings happiness and enjoyment to the lives of people. Of Chinese descent embedded with a small mix of European blood, he migrated to Australia in 1984 with his parents from Hong Kong. He draws inspiration from music, sports, nature, space and religion. Wanting to create a better world was the key motivation to study practical science. After graduating from the University of Melbourne in 2003 with two degrees in the Bachelor of Engineering as well as the Bachelor of Science, he worked in a variety of industries including aerospace, banking, tax and social security. He now lives in Melbourne with his wife and loves sharing his visionary ideas and universal philosophy for a united world.

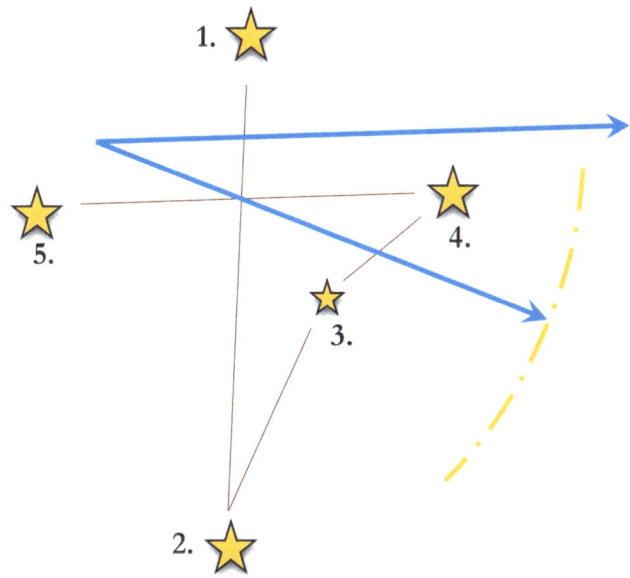

*My star signature is inspired by "The Southern Cross" constellation.
It incorporates a Sagittarius style acute pointing arrows resembling an archer with a bow.
A unique feature is the number and path I used to join the stars together.*

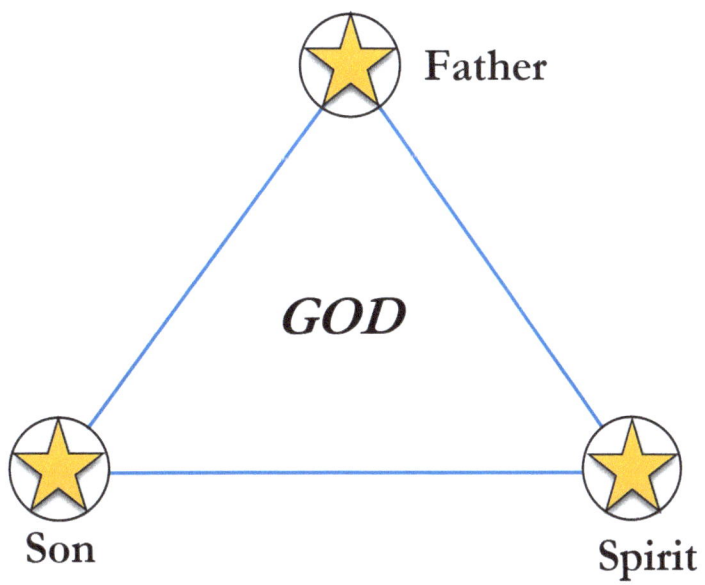

My Universal Anchor is "The Holy Trinity"

www.ingramcontent.com/pod-product-compliance
Lightning Source LLC
Chambersburg PA
CBHW042145290426
44110CB00002B/121